Scrum Agile Software Development Master:

Scrum Guide For Beginners

By

Joseph Joyner

Table of Contents

Scrum Agile Software Development Master: Scrum Guide For Beginners

By Joseph Joyner

First Published, 2014

Printed in the United States of America

Introduction

Scrum is a totally new way to come up with high quality projects. Scrum is defined as a network made of strategic, agile and flexible development techniques used by teams in software projects or products. However with the flexibility of Scrum it may also be used to improve project output in an actual setting. It may be adapted to so many different applications: at school, in business, in company projects and in community projects.

Traditionally, projects or any kind of campaign is finished in a step by step and methodological manner; teams or individuals follow a rigid framework to come up with a finished project. All the exhausted efforts of the teams or individuals that are included in the project are evaluated at the end of the process wherein the finished product or project is assessed. But in a Scrum framework, there is always room for change. There is always a possibility that there may be unpredicted situations that can bring about a change in the project. Therefore, Scrum is all about using an empirical and flexible approach to the fulfillment of any project; teams are constantly called for meetings to discuss the outcome of their specific parts as well as any changes that may be done. Scrum makes projects more systematic and at the same time reduces the possibility of encountering error in the long run. Scrum could be time consuming but results are high quality and very efficient in the end.

Chapter 1. How Does The Scrum Framework Work?

Using Scrum is easy when you understand the framework of the application. Scrum is made of three core roles; understanding these different roles is the first step in learning how Scrum works and how it may be applied to your particular project. These roles are present in every Scrum team and in an online definition of what Scrum is, there are no particular qualifications, job descriptions or careers that qualify for each role.

1. The Product Owner – the owner is the representative of the customer. He sees to it that the team delivers the project with the most quality and on time. He is accountable to the customers as well as the team since he provides the financial aspect of the project. Without the project owner there will be no one to fund the project and there will be no project well. The product owner however may also be a member of the production team and may also be doing other jobs in the team to ensure that products are delivered according to the customers' specifications.

2. The Development Team – these are the actual people that are working on a project and they are responsible in the delivery of shippable products to the customer at the end of each project. In the creation of software or applications, members of a development team may include people with different skills and talents. Members of the team may range from 5 to 10 and each member may be in charge of analysis, designing, developing, testing, and documentation and so on. Bigger and more complex projects have a development team composed of smaller teams. For instance there could be 5 smaller teams that make up a development team and a small team may be in charge of design, analysis, development and so on. Each team is represented by a team leader and these report to Scrum masters in every team meeting; all the teams along with their respective members are invited to join team meetings but usually their team representatives are the ones that report to the Scrum master.

3. The Scrum Master – the Scrum master is like a project leader or coordinator that keeps things in order. He takes in a lot of responsibilities; he must coordinate Scrum meetings, eliminate distractions so that teams or the team is able to focus on their goals, he facilitates meetings and tries to find any potential challenges and improvements for the project.

Each role is interdependent on each role and learning how each of these roles function is important in the fulfilment of any type of project. It is also worth knowing that in an actual Scrum framework, certification is available to fully teach each member of the Scrum team about their specific tasks. Certification increases the knowledge of Scrum masters and their project developers on how Scrum is done effectively and to use it in different applications. Certification is done in online and offline training centers.

What are some useful tips on how to use Scrum?

In order to be very productive in using Scrum, there are strategies that may be used. As mentioned, anyone may use this framework to come up with efficient and high quality outcomes or projects.

Chapter 2. Scrum Vocabulary

Possibly the best way to improve your productivity through the use of Scrum is to understand the basic vocabulary that people that promote the framework use. You should also try to use it as often as you can. The terms are common in all Scrum users and it is advised that anyone or any organization or business that would like to adapt Scrum take by heart these terms and use these accordingly.

A few basic terms that you MUST learn and use:

1. Sprint – this is Scrum's term for a 30-day effort of a Scrum team to fulfil their goals/projects or any required output.

2. Product backlog – this is a list of requirements or it may be comparable to a to-do list. It may be a daily list or a weekly list or it may even be a sprint backlog but all in all these only have one aim and that is to organize the team or members of the Scrum team about their roles. When an item is included in a product backlog list, it means that it has to be done at once.

3. Sprint backlog – as mentioned it is a type of backlog; it is a list that includes items with the highest priority from the product backlog list

4. Scrum team – is made of the product owner, the Scrum master and the development team. It may be a small team composed of 5 members or may be as complicated as 9 or more members. Technically may be several teams in a development team and these may vary according to the industry or the type of project or outcome being done.

5. Scrum process- this is the usual way Scrum is done. It starts with creating a backlog to the fulfilment of the goal or the delivery of the finished product.

6. Sprint burn down chart – this is a progress of a sprint according to its length. The progress may be plotted daily as meetings are done daily and as the project moves on and the outcome is ready to be presented or shipped, the burn down chart is accomplished regularly even several times in a day.

7. Spike – a spike is defined as a time-boxed period wherein the team does research, brain storms for concepts and create project studies or prototypes of a project. Spikes may be in the beginning of any project or in between sprints. Usually, sprints are done in an effort to expand the knowledge of the development team, to secure budget approvals and to prepare the team for the actual project. The duration of a spike may be agreed upon by the project owner and the

Scrum manager; the time for a spike is followed very well regardless of the fulfilment of any objective for the activity.

8. Daily Scrum meeting – these are meetings that include the members of the development team and this is done daily for about 15 minutes. The meeting ends on the particular time regardless if the goal or the goals of the meeting was discussed. The limited time for Scrum meetings actually trains people the importance of time management and that overlooking even a second of precious Scrum meeting time could be very costly in the fulfilment of their goals.

9. Sprint planning – this is the period wherein the product owner and the rest of the team create a sprint goal. All the items are considered in planning and the goal is to organize a sprint goal that every member of the team is comfortable with.

10. Sprint review – this is checking on the progress of a sprint in relevance to the sprint goal.

11. Sprint retrospective meeting – compare this to debriefing wherein the Scrum master along with the team discover anything that must be changed on the next sprint.

12. Impediments – these are any kind of obstacle or challenge that can affect the productivity of a development team. These are acknowledged by the team along with all the members; and along with determining and acknowledging the presence of these impediments, a feasible solution is also determined.

13. PBI or product backlog item – this is the actual work described in work units that was completed in a sprint.

14. Release – this is the time when the product or the finished project has been released to the customer as stated in a contract or from a particular marketplace obligation

15. Velocity – this is the amount of product backlog that the Scrum team can handle in a sprint. Technically the higher the velocity the more efficient the Scrum team is and the lower the velocity the less efficient the team is. However there are several reasons for the increase or decrease in the velocity of a Scrum team; the complexity of the project and the expertise of the development team as well as other factors may all affect the velocity.

16. Abnormal termination – there are times when a project owner cancels a sprint; there are many reasons why a sprint or a project is cancelled. It may be due to poor work out put, poor compliance to the sprint goals, problems with finances and so many more.

Chapter 3. Scrum Process

The Scrum process is a step by step way of looking at how Scrum works. Take note that using Scrum is very organized and time-bounded. Almost all activities and meetings are highly timed and this somehow increases productivity in a team.

1. Backlog creation – this is the time when the product owner and the Scrum team meet. Their agenda is to discuss the creation of a product backlog as well as a sprint backlog. The vision of the project is discussed by the project owner since he represents the customer; he knows exactly what the customer expects and when it is expected to happen.

2. Sprint planning – this is an initial meeting that happens after the product backlog is created. There are two phases of a sprint planning and the initial phase is all about reiterating the product backlog while the second phase involves the Scrum team selecting the items that need to be completed in a sprint. Based on the expertise of the team, selecting the items on top priority is also done during the second phase of the sprint planning step.

3. Creation of a sprint schedule – as the priority items are settled by the development team a sprint schedule is formulated. The priority items are further broken down into smaller, feasible tasks and these are assigned to each member of the team. In more complicated projects, tasks are assigned according to the abilities, skills or talents of each team.

4. Sprint starts – as mentioned a sprint may last from 15 to 30 days. The product backlog and the sprint backlog are completed and there are no other items added to the backlog. A sprint may only start when a schedule is formed and actual tasks are distributed.

5. Daily Scrum – these are daily 15 minute meetings that are usually composed of reports that are based on what they have done after the most recent daily Scrum. After the meeting the Scrum master will take note of any issues and to look for the ideal solution for each issue. Daily meetings are the highlight of a Scrum framework because the proponents of Scrum agree that a team is strengthened with constant interaction and that issues may be settled before these become costly errors through this manner as well. The Scrum master announces Scrum meetings on a specific time each day and these must be attended by every member of the development team but only the team representative or leader reports. Any changes are announced during daily

Scrums especially any changes that the customer wants to implement, changes in the release dates and so on.

6. Sprint review – to cap every sprint, a review is done. A review is all about sharing what has happened in a previous sprint, accepting suggestions and announcing changes in the next sprints and any other important details that members have to be aware of.

7. After a review - is the announcement of a new task or project by the project manager. He calls the Scrum manager and the development team to create another backlog and the process begins.

Chapter 4. Improve Your Scrum Environment

Scrum is not limited to the development of software or computer applications, it is a very flexible framework that may also be used in projects for different industries, offices, teams and even in organizing teams for school work. The best way to make the most of Scrum in these different applications is to improve your Scrum environment.

In an office setting

In an office or in any other business, you may introduce Scrum as early as before your next project. Mobile people that will head teams and recommend that they undergo training for Scrum; when you and team leaders are skilled in using Scrum there will be better application of this framework to any project based on your industry.

In an office or company, designate a common meeting place or a daily Scrum venue. Remember that Scrum meetings should be done in the same place and on the same time every day. Your venue should be comfortable as it is adequate enough to accommodate all the members of your team. There should be at least a white board, a computer with access to the web, a projector and a stereo system.

If your team prefers to conduct daily Scrums elsewhere, you should make this venue accessible each day. It must be a private place and a venue with all the mentioned equipment.

In a school setting

Students should be introduced to Scrum as early as possible since it may help them complete projects and school works that require them to work in large groups. Scrum will help students work in an efficient, well-organized and time bounded manner. Same as in an office setting, members of the academe should be trained in Scrum. Professional training with certification is important and therefore these must be taken by teachers and other personnel involved in motivating students.

When it comes to creating a better environment where students could work on a Scrum framework, a suitable venue should be provided with all the necessary equipment. Scrum may be integrated in almost all group work activities but the rules should be less strenuous like allowing longer time frame to organize a schedule and to conduct daily Scrums.

In a community setting

Projects of all sorts are common in a community team effort setting. Volunteers may be organized with the use of Scrum in an effort to provide different kinds of community activities like medical missions, relief operations, disaster coordination, clean up drives and recycling drives. Since most community projects are done in a limited number of time, the creation of a sprint is done in a flexible manner as well. A community center could be designated as a proper venue for a daily scrum and it is greatly encouraged to do so since reports of what is currently being done and being accomplished is important in a community project. Whether the project is as simple as giving gifts to less privileged community members to helping people affected by natural calamity and rehabilitating them Scrum can help.

It could be hard to control or more so improve anyone's environment as you and your team practice Scrum in the community. But since Scrum is flexible it may be adapted to suit the strenuous and stressful community setting as well. The best approach is to educate and certify community leaders and volunteers in the use of Scrum instead.

Chapter 5. Tips During Scrum Meetings

Daily Scrums are done in the same venue and at the same time each day but there are some ways to improve these daily events to make your sprints more achievable. For one people involved in Daily Scrums are not allowed to sit. They are told to stand up and to listen which is why Daily Scrums are often called stand up meetings.

In a meeting the leader of the team should be the only one to stand up and talk and everyone else should listen. The Daily Scrum is not about providing the status of your work but all about what the team is doing and their progress and of course reporting if any hurdles have been experienced in the fulfilment of a sprint backlog.

In a meeting, technical concerns may be discussed afterwards or preferably after the meeting is over. A stand up is provided if there are immediate clarifications regarding any issues of the sprint. The scrum master and the project owner should be made aware of a stand-up as soon as possible.

Chapter 6. How to Influence Your Team

Just like any kind of team or project development strategy, Scrum is dependent on the ability of the scrum master to influence his people. The Scrum master actually has so many things in his hands and one of this is to efficiently influence his people. A team needs constant reassurance of their efforts and their goals which is why the Scrum master has to reiterate these goals with the use of the following strategies.

1. Create a poster of how Scrum is done and what your members can contribute in achieving your Scrum goals. Your poster may feature the various goals that you have in a sprint and the various backlogs that must be considered.

2. By crediting good work of a team or an individual involve in your project, a team manager will be able to influence his team to success. Credits may be appreciated in so many ways; a company recognition from an official site or social media site, giving a cash or equivalent incentive and so many more. Remember that a team is only good when its members are able to perform well.

3. Give credit and focus on the smallest improvements. Just like providing credit to anyone that deserves it, focusing on small improvements could help increase the output of any

team. For instance scrum masters should focus on the abilities of a team that was able to increase its work output and to finish their backlogs on time. Creators of Scrum understand that it is very important to highlight the accomplishments of a team at all times.

Chapter 7. Improve Your Technical Knowledge

Scrum has been primarily developed for the creation and the development of software and therefore the need to improve your company or team's technical knowledge in your field can do a lot of wonders to make Scrum effective. For instance you are the Scrum master of a team and apart from following the Scrum framework you seem to find that there are still more mistakes when it comes to the quality of products that affects delivery of your finished product release. You conduct a sprint review revealing that your team lacks the skills and technical knowledge in handling a work order. Training should be done as soon as possible to reduce costly errors that may eventually lead to customers losing trust in your abilities and skills.

Having poor technical knowledge in the application of Scrum may also jeopardize your projects and therefore undergoing courses and training is important. Project owners especially scrum masters need to become certified to handle teams for Scrum as well. Getting technical knowledge about your industry may be done online and through offline courses while Scrum certification training may only be provided by accredited training centers and online sites.

Chapter 8. Limitations of Scrum

There are also several limitations of Scrum and learning these should make you more efficient in handling any type of project and joining Scrum teams. Although it is flexible for different industries, Scrum may not be widely accepted considering that it is a radical, time boxed and very idealistic approach in doing projects. Some businesses, especially companies run by older generations may not be in favour of using a very limited time frame. They may still want to stick to discussing every little aspect of a project and to devote as much time in creating rather than hurrying to make it to a deadline.

Although Scrum may be implemented in an office or workplace there is still no guarantee that every employee agrees to its use. Some may want to work on a project according to their own ways and hurrying could only lead to serious complications in the quality outcome of a product.

Scrum is an effective approach to getting a project or a goal done right and of course offers a lot of flexibility since daily meetings is done to take care of any hurdle that can affect the productivity of a team. There may be limitations to its use especially to older generations but it is never too late to learn a new approach to project management. New and established companies are using Scrum and have been getting great results.

Chapter 9. Using IP Communications Technology

With the use of latest technology Daily Scrums are now possible even when other members of your team are from other parts of the world. IP technology can help you efficiently conduct daily meetings and will even get you to compromise on backlogs in a more efficient manner. A tip is to designate a particular time of day where all your members are comfortable in meeting each other through IP calling. There are free IP services like Skype and Yahoo where you can hold daily meetings. You may also use latest technology to deal with Sprints. For instance you can use IP technology to post messages or for project managers to talk to team leaders and vice versa. Work is best done when everything is synchronized and you can do this with the use of latest in communications technology.

You may also use other online technology to boost your Daily Scrums like using MMS messages, using video calling, using presentation software and so many more. Certainly the web has made it possible for any business use Scrum for enhancing their productivity. And possibly what's best about using all these latest technologies is that you may meet with your Scrum team anywhere you are even with the use of a mobile computing device.

Chapter 10. Using Scrum for Future Business Projects

Scrum may be used as a mainstay of your project planning and project management regardless of what products or services you offer. There are a lot of advantages in the use of Scrum and one of these is increased customer satisfaction. As they say in every business, the customer is always right.

When your customers receive their products on time and at the highest quality you will be able to guarantee that your business will get more consumer acceptance, you will have increased revenue in the long run and better brand recognition. By utilizing an efficient strategy in mobilizing teams for any project, you will certainly be able to overcome any kind of project or goal. And if your business does not recognize the value of Scrum then it is never too late to make this a part of your workplace. Scrum certification may be done online and offline according to the learner's preference.

Thank You Page

I want to personally thank you for reading my book. I hope you found information in this book useful and I would be very grateful if you could leave your honest review about this book. I certainly want to thank you in advance for doing this.

www.ingramcontent.com/pod-product-compliance
Lightning Source LLC
Chambersburg PA
CBHW071554080326
40690CB00056B/2036